Network Marketing Truth

Jac Hodges

Alison
keep going!
Jac x

DEDICATION

Well there are three special people who will get mentioned in this
dedication but a whole host of other people who have been there on the
journey with me, you know who you are!
But the most important three people in my life are the Hodges pack, the
pack that has always got my back
So, this is for you Christian, Jacob & Oliver
Thanks for all the years tolerating me working as much as I do and ranting
when I needed to. I truly couldn't have done any of it without you guys

Find out more about Jac at www.jachodges.online

TRUTH BOMBS

1. Truth Bomb One - What the hell is network marketing anyway?

2. Truth Bomb Two - How do I choose the right company for me?

3. Truth Bomb Three - It's time to get serious about your business!

4. Truth Bomb Four - How to Build your Personal Sales

5. Truth Bomb Five – Getting your life balance right

6. Truth Bomb Six – How to slay your Social Media

7. Truth Bomb Seven - Become a Leader you would follow

8. Truth Bomb Eight– How to handle the Unethical bulls**t

9. Truth Bomb Nine – How to analyse your business

10. Truth Bomb Ten – Go forth and multiply

It's time to go all in!

Network Marketing Truth

Firstly, let me tell you about me.

I wouldn't like to say how many books I have read over the years on Network Marketing

The one thing most have in common is a vast proportion of them spend the first section telling you how amazing the author is. I'll apologise now for those that I offend but I find most completely self-indulgent and they spend a good proportion of time telling you how incredible the author is and often they don't actually give you much of a strategy to follow, it's mostly just waffle.

The answers in the most part are not in these books, you may get a few ideas, but it often doesn't set you a plan to follow.

Now I'm not saying I have all the answers either, but I am willing to share what I have learnt along my Network Marketing journey in an honest, no holds barred way. This might just give you the head start you're looking for if you are new to the industry and maybe help you avoid some of the pitfalls that people go through in the early days.

Or if you are already established in the industry it might help you get your business out of a rut. Maybe you are just looking for a bit of inspiration if you have already been in the biz for a while and feel like you don't quite know what to do next. Maybe you were sold the dream, but you just can't seem to make it work in the way your upline promised.

My time is precious and so is yours so let's cut to the chase.

My journey is as simple as this.

I'm a mum and have had a successful career in Network Marketing. I have experience of the self-employed, corporate employed and Consultative route in this industry. I have not just built successful teams in the industry once with one brand, but I have done it several times over in both Global companies and brand-new start-ups.

That's pretty much all you need to know about me, you've already picked my book up, so I don't need to sell myself to you. You've taken a punt on me already and for that I salute you, you little action taker you.

What I hope you get from this book is a blueprint for you to go and follow to find your own way to success as after all YOU are the magic ingredient to making this shiz work.

I adore Network Marketing, it's my great passion in life and I am highly protective of it's reputation so I am going to share everything I have learnt along the way, warts and all! It will hopefully set you on a wonderful, exciting, roller coaster of a new career.

However, a word of warning if you have picked this book up and are expecting it to fix everything for you without you putting the work in. Step away from it immediately, I mean it, put it down and go focus on your paid job instead.

This industry is tough, and you have to do the graft for it to work for you.

The books you read only work if you do, it's 'Self-help' not 'Shelf-help' so implement what you learn, don't read this book and stick it back on the on the shelf to collect dust.

I have watched many people over the years succeed in this business but have watched more fail because they didn't put the work in consistently and ultimately the buck stops with you. You make a choice where your journey takes you. This book can help you but only if you are willing to read it, digest it but more importantly go and take massive, intentional ACTION.

The industry has taken a bit of a battering in the last few years in the media and on Social Media however my personal believe is this industry is amazing and anyone can be successful in it, how amazing is that, literally anyone and that includes YOU!

I genuinely believe this to be true for you.

We live in a world where, due to the current financial climate, lots of us need a side hustle to achieve the goals we set for ourselves. I believe the younger, millennial generation think about the world and business differently to the older generation. Lots genuinely don't want to settle for working for someone else and want to follow a career as an entrepreneur. They believe this is possible for them in a way we never did. This is a whole different subject, but our educational system is not fit for purpose particularly when it comes to the subject of business. If you are a millennial, reading this book, well done for choosing Network Marketing, it's time to get your hustle on.

If you are not a millennial this industry isn't a get-rich-quick scheme just to be really clear. Of course, some people do make large amounts of money very quickly. Many would say those people are lucky. But success isn't based on luck. Success in this industry is based on following some very basic yet dynamic principles and then repeating them over and over! And then repeating them again long after the motivation to do so has left you.

So pretty much if you have the courage to begin, you can succeed.

If someone else is already doing it successfully, so can YOU!

Ignore the "You have to be in at the start", or the "The company is everywhere, there isn't any potential left". If you have enough passion, laser focus and get super consistent with your income producing activities, this opportunity could be life changing for you and the people your business touches.

Who wouldn't want to be in a business where you only get successful from helping other people get successful? How cool is that?

You don't need to be a genius, have money to invest, be a trainer, a super sales-person, a highly trained manager or have any experience in anything at all to be successful in this industry. All you need is passion and excitement and the ability to learn and think on your feet but most of all you need to be coachable. You must be willing to learn from the people around you.

If you enjoy my book pass it on to someone else that it may help 😊

You CAN have it all
Just not straight away!

Truth Bomb One

WHAT THE HECK IS NETWORK MARKETING ANYWAY?

There are lots of terms used to describe this business,

Network Marketing, Direct Selling, Multi-Level-Marketing, MLM, Relationship Marketing. These terms all mean the same thing. The list goes on with the different terms for it but, in a nutshell, what you are describing is a method of selling direct to the consumer without the need for a retail location (shop). You can do this through various methods such as face to face, parties, through a brochure, social media, online etc.

When you start talking about it being multi-level you are simply talking about building a team underneath you that you earn from, that hopefully, grows in width and depth as you develop both customers and team members.

It's not a new concept, the original direct sellers started in the 18 hundreds and are still going today, so it must be a system that works, right?

The term MLM (Multi-Level Marketing) has become surrounded in stories of being a scam or people getting ripped off and has become the term used to describe the pushier companies in the direct sales industry. There are also lots of businesses that think they are not MLM, however I've got news for you. If your company pays out commission payments for you building your business downwards through "Multi Levels" and pays you commission for doing so you ARE in Multi-Level Marketing (MLM).

So, get over the term as it just describes a business model, not the way the business is conducted. I am always shocked when leaders of top global businesses argue this point – get over yourselves, it's just a term.

Whatever you call the business you are in; the principal is the same for most direct sales businesses. You sell personally and encourage other people to do the same . You earn from your own personal sales and earn a percentage of commission from the efforts of a team you find and recruit underneath you. Meaning there is no ceiling to your business, you can just keep cloning yourself to sell more product as a team.

Is it the same as a Pyramid Scheme?

You'll get asked this a lot *"Is it like one of those pyramid scheme things"*.

First up, forgive their ignorance and then give them a little bit of education in the nicest possible way. Don't get annoyed, don't get defensive. Simply offer them some education.

I always describe it to them this way.

If you drew out any business what would it look like?

A CEO, a small team of directors, a larger sales team and probably an even larger manufacturing and distribution team. If you drew it out it would be shaped like a triangle/pyramid with far less people at the top than the bottom? Are you employed by somebody? Do you work for a pyramid scheme then?

Pyramid Schemes (sometimes called Ponzi Schemes) were made illegal as they had no product involved, they were just people buying into a concept and the people at the top got very rich without moving a single product. It was selling a concept that promised riches, but left people broke. I can see why people would mistake our industry as being the same, but it isn't as you are basically using a distribution network of like-minded people to reach out to as many customers as you can.

Providing product is changing hands and you are earning from the volume that is being sold, it's not the same thing at all. Pyramid schemes are illegal so clearly thousands of us would not be involved in them, would we? Never react to this question from people. Just explain how Network Marketing works and move on.

The sad fact is that the odd pyramid scheme does rear its ugly head, even here in the UK. If you join a pyramid selling scheme, you're likely to lose your money. If you promote, or operate one you could go to prison!

The simple way to tell – do you and your team sell products?

Don't take
constructive criticism
from someone who
hasn't constructed
anything

Network Marketing has had some bad press!

You will be surrounded by people who don't get why you have started a Network Marketing business, and that's fine.

In the beginning you will be doing a lot for little return but if you keep consistent, eventually that scale will tip, and you will be doing little for a BIG reward. Most people just aren't tenacious enough to get out the other side. Are you?

You may have people in your inner circle that don't get what you are doing, and again this is fine but be ready to be criticised for joining Network Marketing. The key is to block any of this negativity out and understand that their fear of you starting your business comes from caring about you but not always from understanding the industry . The people around you have your best interests at heart but often have little or no Network Marketing experience so of course they are not the best people to be giving you advice. Also watch out for the people in your life who have tried Network Marketing and had a bad experience. They can really get under your skin in terms of knocking your confidence about your decision. If they tried and failed in the industry there will be a reason for that; they may have some horror stories to tell you (trust me there are some pretty bad ones out there!) but their journey is not yours. they may not have had the right support, knowledge or sheer grit to make this thing work for them so of course they now have a negative opinion.

The media in recent years has given the industry a real kicking and don't get me wrong, some of what you hear is true, but lots of it is very one sided and is coming from disgruntled ex-Network Marketers that just didn't make it.

You can listen to the bad press or you can choose to become part of the solution to change people's perception of the industry. As I said at the very beginning, I am still hugely passionate about the industry and the opportunity it offers to everyone who has the balls to explore it.

When you join you may not have the skills you need to succeed but that is then your job to learn and develop the skills you do need to make it work.

Make sure you put everything you learn into ACTION though. Boy have I watched lots that are obsessed with personal development, attend all the meetings and then go away and do diddly squat with what they just learnt.

Promise me this will not be you?

Commit to your business, trust in the process and go and take massive, intentional action.

I want to see you become part of the statistic that changes the perception of the industry not one that falls by the wayside.

Buckle up, get ready to learn and challenge yourself more than you ever have before but most of all enjoy the ride in this awesome industry.

Will it always go smoothly, hell no! You are probably going to be challenged more than you ever have been, but you can also build a business that most people can only dream of.

Go with your gut instinct
It is rarely wrong

Truth Bomb Two

HOW DO I CHOOSE THE RIGHT COMPANY FOR ME?

Now this piece of the jigsaw is very important.

Do not rush this part of the process. There are literally hundreds of companies and brands vying for your attention and for you to join up with them. If you are new to the industry use the form in a few pages to analyse the companies you are interested in to whittle down your shortlist to a winner.

This is also relevant if you are already with a business, it's time to check you are with the right one. Follow the questions as though you are looking at the industry as a brand-new person if you are already with a company.

First off, do you already know people in Network Marketing?

Approach these people with caution, they have an agenda and will be trying to get you to join their team. Their opportunity will in their opinion be the best one out there, however it may not be right for you so it's about getting an unbiased view on their company. It sometimes feels safer to join a brand that you already have a friend in, however don't be afraid to go it alone and choose the business that fits you both in terms of the brand and the products.

Product is key, you HAVE to love the product you are representing, or it just isn't going to work for you. Your passion for the products will become infectious and people will find that hard to resist.

Trust me, I've been there not loving the product I was representing! If you don't wear make-up don't try and sell it, if you're not into health it's pointless you trying to sell health products.

You get the gist.

Start doing your research online and on social media. Visit the company website, what is your first impression? Does what it is saying resonate in some way with you. Visit the corporate Facebook page, how many people are following them, are there reviews. Start to make your shortlist of companies that interest you.

Next up, place an order if you have not used their products before. You're looking to find out what their service is like. Did someone personally contact you? Often your order placed directly through the company will be passed to a self-employed Consultant, did they contact you? Were you kept informed about the progress of your order? How long did it take to arrive? Did you love the products when you used them? Be honest with yourself about what you really think.

Check that the company's values align with your personal moral compass. Try and find out what the culture of the business is like and make sure it resonates with you.

Is their mission statement on their website? Be warned though this doesn't always mean a lot. I know a lot of big corporations with great mission statements that do the exact opposite of what their statement promises. However, it should give you a bit of an idea of what the business 'should' be about. Check that things that are important to you are present. Are they cruelty free if that's important to you? Are they global? Can you sell internationally and across borders. Where do their ingredients come from? Are they ethically producing their products, could there be supply chain issues in the future depending on where or how they are manufacturing? I have come across this one with a brand I loved and put my heart and soul into but ultimately they couldn't get their supply chain right so eventually I couldn't put my name or my results to it. They started letting their customers, Consultants and Leaders down due to horrendous manufacturing errors. Where do they manufacture? These are all things that may have a bearing on the future of this business and whether this company is the right fit for you.

Be weary of the new, shiny companies that spring up. I'm not saying don't join a brand-new Network Marketing biz but I have seen lots fall by the wayside, so just be aware that it may be less secure than a longer established business.

Get hold of their compensation/commission plan.

Break it down and get to grips with how it works. Is it so complicated you can't make head nor tail of it? This is never a good sign! Does it seem impossible to earn a decent amount or does it seem ridiculously easy and over generous, again this is never a good sign. What extra incentives do they run and do these seem doable. It's sometimes hard when you're new in this business to understand a company's comp plan. Find someone to explain it if needs be and keep revisiting and asking questions until you understand it fully.

Finally speak to some people already in the business, choose a mixture of people so the super successful ones, the ones who have just joined, what was the training and support like?

Will you just be signed and abandoned?
What support will you be offered to help you get up and running? Will you be supported to build a business with longevity?

Try and find out what the retention rate of the business is for their self-employed Consultants, do people stay with them?
If everyone that joins leaves as quickly as they joined, there's an issue. However, this also goes the other way, if you can only find people that have been in the business for 20+ years this business could potentially be old fashioned and not forward thinking enough for you.

Find out whether the people already in the business are expected to purchase a lot of product for themselves.
If you join and they instantly encourage you to change every product in your home to theirs, be wary. Never a good sign.

Is the starter kit or join up fee reasonably priced?
Lots of companies make their money purely from the amount of sign ups they get, they don't really mind whether it works for you or not as you've bought your kit and that is where their dosh comes from.

What price are promotional materials to support your business?
What promotional materials will you need to run your business if any. This will form your running costs for your business so make sure whatever you need is not wildly expensive.

Do they insist you grow a team, or do they leave the pace you grow up to you?
Watch out for the companies that encourage you to aggressively grow a team.

Do you have to pay any annual fees for website/email/social assets etc.
If you have to pay an annual fee which is quite normal by the way, what is included? Does it seem like good value for what you are getting?

Use the quick guide on the next page to shortlist your potential companies. Once you have made this short list of companies how do you finally decide which company to go with?

Shortlist Company 1	Shortlist Company 2	Shortlist Company 3
Brand	Brand	Brand
Joining Fee £	Joining Fee £	Joining Fee £
Love Products YES NO	Love Products YES NO	Love Products YES NO
Are there any annual fees? YES NO Cost £	Are there any annual fees? YES NO Cost £	Are there any annual fees? YES NO Cost £
Love Company Ethics YES NO	Love Company Ethics YES NO	Love Company Ethics YES NO
Know people in biz YES NO	Know people in biz YES NO	Know people in biz YES NO
Placed an order, how was it?	Placed an order, how was it?	Placed an order, how was it?
Personal Sales Commission From % to %	Personal Sales Commission From % to %	Personal Sales Commission From % to %
Additional Team Commission From % to %	Additional Team Commission From % to %	Additional Team Commission From % to %

Does doing more than one MLM at a time work?

In my opinion 'No'! But I would love it if you prove me wrong.

If you are going to make a sustainable business, you need to commit to what you are building. I see network marketers' flit from company to company because they either fall out of love with where they were or worse still there are people who are addicted to the buzz of starting again from the beginning and get hooked into the next BIG thing every time. They go after the next shiny new thing and abandon the business they were with as quickly as they came in.

However, what I will say is sometimes you can choose the wrong company first time round when you're new to MLM, and you then find something further down the line that fits more authentically with you, that's ok. Make a move if you have to, but approach with caution as your network can be left feeling very confused when your first company was the best thing since sliced bread when you joined it, but now you have a brand new band wagon you've jumped on. They may not always be up for following you so proceed with caution.

Do your homework right first time round and only make a move if you really have to.

Is Party Plan still relevant?

Now this is an interesting one.

Back in the day there were hundreds of businesses working very successfully in the Party Plan format. You know the format. Inviting your friends' round to view a product demo and purchase from their brochure. The host normally gets rewarded for having their friends' round.

Now, I do believe there is still a place for Party Plan however I also believe it has to adapt to an omni channel version. Make sure if you join a conventional Party Plan business that they have the technology in place to support a multi-channel approach.

It has to be both an online and offline offering now in my opinion.

We all live ridiculously busy lives and have little free time to spare. The days of the stay at home housewife and mother are pretty much all but gone. Most couples require both of you to work to just survive and therefore to organise having friends' round to support a stranger's business is a big ask.

We also become very conscious and feel slightly uncomfortable about our friends feeling they have to make the "sympathy purchase" for us when they attend. To make this format work you have to be a great networker and maybe there are easier ways for you to generate sales?

Think about whether you will feel comfortable asking people to organise these types of events for you. I have seen this done very well and I have also seen it done really badly when people want to run for the hills every time they see their party plan friend coming for fear of having the life hassled out of them to book a date with them. Desperation is never a good look.

It is really important if you run this type of Network Marketing business that you come at it from the angle of what is in it for your hosts. Make sure they know what they will get out of it and make them feel super appreciated.

My advice is also to develop an offline/online strategy so that people can either attend or get involved online if that is their preferred method of shopping. It's about how does the consumer want to shop – not how do you want to sell to them.

Customer service is always king so make sure you are forming long lasting, meaningful relationships with your hosts and guests, so they want to regularly either attend or host for you.

Consider developing a Social Media version of your party, Facebook live is awesome for you to demo your products. You can then tap into your network and your connections network really easily. There are over 2 billion monthly Facebook users why would you not tap into that! We all have different friends on our Social Media so if you get it right you have an opportunity to tap into your friend's network too. Think about your online party the same as an offline party and you can make this method work.

It's really important that you ensure you connect with everyone you party with on Social Media after the event so they never forget where you are and can see all up and coming offers. Don't just party and run. Form long lasting relationships that have meaning, offer value and great customer service.

See below my blueprint for hosting a successful Online party format:

Step One:

Find your Online host. This is not about you hosting your own Facebook party over and over. It's not a bad thing to start with your own. This is really bout you tapping into other people's networks – the same as you would in the real world. You wouldn't just keep hosting a home party over and over at your own house?

Step Two:

Provide your Host with a nice inviting image to share and set them the task of inviting 10-20 close friends to your Facebook event. These invites should be sent out either by Text or WhatsApp not via Facebook. This is about them inviting the people who are closest to them. If they were going to host a party in the 'Real' world, these would be the people they would invite. Ensure they don't go on Facebook and just invite everyone. Trust me when I say the more connected to them the guests are, the more engaged the party will be. Smaller events ALWAYS work better.

Step Three:

Host coaching is really important. Help your host to identify and connect with what she wants to get out of the event. Is there an item she would like to get for free? Make sure you make it really clear that she will need to engage with the event, send reminders and engage with it on Facebook.

Step Four:

Set Up the Facebook event. Invite your Host to be a Co-Host and get her to invite the people that she invited by Text and WhatsApp. Get her to send a little reminder Text/WhatsApp to say the Facebook Event is set up and they should have received an invite so they don't miss it in their notifications.

Step Five:

Create curiosity in the Facebook Event in the run up to your Live demo. This is not about giving all the information away. Do not be tempted to product vomit on the Guests. I know you love your products and company but if you share all the info at this point people will make a decision based on that info instead of based on hearing and connecting with you. People buy from people, not from businesses.

Step Six:

Go Live in the Facebook Event at a pre-arranged time. Get the Host to send her Guests another little reminder beforehand so you do have some Guests attending. Showcase both the products and your business Opportunity. Make sure you include how to order with you.

Step Seven:
Follow up with everyone who was invited. Message individually and try and open a dialogue, something along the lines of 'Thanks so much for attending XXXXX's party, which of the products I showcased was your favourite?''. Answer any questions and queries. Don't forget to ask if they would like to host their own Event.

Step Eight:
Close the event. Don't leave the event hanging. Post to say when the event will be finishing and when orders need to be in by along with what the Host got from hosting for you.

Growth isn't meant to be comfortable

Truth Bomb Three

IT'S TIME TO GET SERIOUS ABOUT YOUR BUSINESS

You've joined your top short-listed company, now what?

The most important thing you need to understand before you begin is you have just started a business, yep little old you is now a 'Business Owner'. And it is just that - A business!

It's not a get rich scheme, no-one is going to do the work for you and it's absolutely NOT going to happen by accident. It's going to take hard work, sweat and sometimes tears to get this up and running. It's not for the faint hearted, it will test you and you will often feel like it's plain old not worth it.

What you do on the tough days is what will get you through – not what you do when it is going well. That's the reality so when I said this guide would be warts and all, I meant it; it is pointless me sugar coating it.

You will 100% need to find extra time in your schedule, sometimes your partner/family won't like this.

Don't let your upline fool you into thinking building a business from your phone with a few minutes here and there is going to cut the mustard. If they tell you this they are not being truthful with you.

You will almost definitely spend a lot of time in the early days convincing people of why you are doing this.

You will also probably feel a lot in the early days that your effort does not match your reward. But what you do at the start is what will make the difference. If you let other people's opinions cloud your mindset, your business is doomed. Don't take constructive criticism from people around you that actually haven't ever constructed anything! So, unless the people around you offering advice are million-pound Network Marketers, or highly talented entrepreneurs in their own right, I wouldn't listen to them. Shut some of this noise out as it will not help your journey to listen to it.

You will need to be more persistent and tenacious than you have EVER been in your life.

You will need to take MASSIVE intentional action. And let's face it taking action can be really scary. Sitting in the security and safety of your life now is probably easier – right?

There will 100% be the possibility of failure, it's hard creating new routines and who really has the time to start a new venture in this already crazy life we all lead? Feeling like this or saying any of this to yourself is perfectly normal. You may make some other BS excuses to yourself to keep you in your nice cosy, comfort zone. Trust me nothing awesome lives there.

Here are some things you may be saying to yourself right now which will ultimately hold you back.

"I need more information before I start"

It's natural to want to know as much as you can about something before you start, and there's no benefit to going into something half-cocked and not having all the info however you'll learn much, much more from actually DOING something than you will from learning about it from other people.

"Maybe I'll really get started tomorrow, next week, next month, next year........"

There will never be a perfect time to start this thing. Tomorrow, next week, or even next year will always seem like a more appealing time to start, but the truth is, NOW is the best time to get cracking.

"I'm not sure it will work"

I'll be honest there will never be a 100% guarantee it will work out for you but you sure as hell won't know unless you try! It's always tempting to put things off, but it's also the first habit you need to break if you want to stop talking about doing amazing things and actually start doing them. ACTION is essential.

The reality is you will probably need at least 3-4 years to build something worth having. Approximately 10% of Network Marketers actually significantly change their life with their business.

Yep, you heard me right 90% of people fail in this business or at least don't make the big time in it. In my opinion the main reason it doesn't work for lots is they just give up too soon due to having unrealistic expectations of how long it will take. How many "conventional" new businesses even turn a profit in year one. Not many I can tell you now.

Be the 10%, come into this with your eyes open about what it will take to make it.

Get a fire in your belly and get to work – EVERY DAY. No one lacks motivation, they lack vision and perspective. Keep your vision at the fore front of your mind.

Get your mindset right from day one and treat your business like a business from day one. Write down all the commitments that you have in your week now. The absolute non-negotiables.

Where are the gaps that you can find the extra time to spend on your business? Commit to these time slots and take intentional action that moves your business forward in this time. Don't fool yourself that 10 mins here and there is going to build an empire – no matter what some of the muppets in the industry might be telling you. This is not going to get built with a few mins here and a few mins there. And if you think it is again, I suggest you step away from my book right now!

It is probably going to mean going through some hardship for the first couple of years. Getting up earlier, going to bed later, not watching your favourite TV shows and doing whatever you need to do to hustle your way to the top.

However, the one thing I do want you to remember is family comes first, I speak from experience when I say I have missed countless milestones in my children's life due to the journey I was on. This isn't ok and if I could have my time again, I am not sure I would have made the same choices. Don't make my mistake and make sure you always put your family's needs first and work your business round that.

You're probably going to have to do some 'stuff' that scares you and that's ok too. That means you are growing!

There are some key tasks that I want you to commit to doing. Refer back to this list regularly and make sure you are completing each one with commitment and consistency.

1: Be a product of your product
2: Speak to your upline every week
3: Complete some sort of personal development every week
4: Gain 2 new customers every month
5: Get 2 new recruits every month
6: Attend your company events

Use the form on the next page to work out which commitments are set in stone each week so i.e. Work, Clubs, activities etc. Then fill in what hours you will dedicate to your business – and stick to it until your circumstances allow you to do more. Put the hours you will work in your diary as though it is a job. Do NOT miss this slot in favour of doing something else; you have to commit to your business and you have to be consistent in the time you have.

	Monday	Tuesday	Wednesday	Thursday	Friday
6am				
7am				
8am				
9am				
10am				
11am				
Noon				
1pm				
2pm				
3pm				
4pm				
5pm				
6pm				
7pm				
8pm				
9pm				
10pm				

Be a Goal Digger

Goal setting and visualisation

Dream BIG my beauties - if you don't start out by dreaming big, you're never going to move beyond mediocrity!

However, having a huge dream can also be a bit overwhelming. After all, when you're dreaming of doing something that's gigantic and so far from your life now, how do you even know where to start?

Here are my top tips to start you off:

1: Get really clear on what you are trying to achieve. Visualisation can help to get you started.

2: Reverse engineer your plan. It sounds a bit strange but start with the big plan and then work it backwards.

3: Find an accountability buddy. Find someone you can check in with every days. Maybe text 3 things you have achieved that have moved you forwards plus 3 things to be grateful for each day.

4: Measure your progress consistently.

Have you ever tried visualisation?

Now I will tell you a story about this subject – I never really got the whole visualisation piece. Goal setting I completely got; make your long-term goal and then break it down into the bitesize chunks that will take you to your ultimate goal, that makes sense to everyone right but I could never really understand visualisation.

The first time I sat in a visualisation session I'll be honest I thought what a crock! Everyone cutting out pictures of what they wanted, setting quite frankly ridiculous goals in my opinion in most cases. It all seemed a bit Blue Peter and definitely too Woo Woo for me and my practical head.

The first time I finally worked on a vision board I made the same mistake and set massive goals that I couldn't really comprehend happening and didn't believe in.

However, there is absolutely a place for visualisation in your business if done the right way. What I did discover really early on was that it is a great exercise to work out what is REALLY important to you, which is often not what you maybe think is important to you. It highlighted to me that my family are actually my biggest driver, that I want location freedom so working for someone else and being employed just doesn't really work for me.

You have to know what your 'Perfect' life looks like to know where to start.

What is important to you?
Where do you see yourself across the next year or longer?
What are your non-negotiables?

Your vision board should inspire you on the shitiest of days and make you keep going because your vision is so strongly resonating with your core. However, I have also learnt that I needed a handful of really tangible goals on there that I can then break down into smaller actions to take me there and trust me you don't have to have all the answers on how you will get there.

If you have the answers on how to achieve all your goals they are quite frankly too small and I wouldn't even bother. Your goals should force you to level up, to strive for new things, to learn more, to become more and to serve more.

So, my advice to you if you have never made one before is to start by working out what really matters to you?

Where do you want to live and with who?
What does your prefect work life look like?
Who will you help?
What will you do in your free time?
What does your life look and feel like?
What are your non-negotiables?

Then lay this out visually however this works for you. It might be notes, pictures, a mind map., video Whatever works for you and gets you fired up put it somewhere that you can see it while you are working. Mine sits behind my desk so when I am in the office it smacks me in the face all day, every day.

You also need to goal set within your business consistently every month and by this I mean the more practical goal setting that takes your business from A to B to keep it growing.

What gets measured, gets done is one of my favourite phrases that people probably get sick of hearing me say. It really is true!

Think of your goal setting like having a map for your business. If you have no map you will get lost, it really is that simple.

If I asked you to jump in your car right now and drive to an address in Birmingham but you can't use a Sat Nav or a map. Maybe you would know roughly which direction to head in to get yourself to Birmingham, let's face it – it's in the middle so you are either going upwards or downwards so you could get yourself to Birmingham by following the signs. However, could you get yourself to the specific address, your final destination? You would drive around, not knowing where you're going, taking lots of deviations, wasting time, feeling lost, getting annoyed and ultimately probably not ever reaching your final destination.

This is what running your business without a goal each month feels like. You need to 100% make yourself accountable for your business performance. The buck stops with you, you are the CEO and the creator of everything in your business.

If you have a clear plan you can predict the future of your business

Heard of SMART goals? This strategy absolutely works but mine works a bit differently. Let's face it the corporate version is a bit dull!

S = Sparkly – Your goals should absolutely make your heart sing

M = Mad – Your goals should stretch you and if you say them out loud other people should think you're a little bit mad

A = Achievable – They should stretch you but not be ridiculous. If your goal is, I'll earn a Million pounds next month when you are currently on a thousand pounds that probably isn't going to happen. Just saying.

R = Re-active – if you miss your goal, re-adjust, re-plan and make it happen. If you get part way through the month and it's looking like you are going to miss do not use this is an excuse to right the month off. Do everything you can to react to your goal and manifest it in the month it belongs to

T = Treasure it – Treasure your goals and keep them somewhere you can see them on a daily basis.

There are some key indicators you need to plan each and every month. I want you to set yourself a goal and then track it against the actual figure you achieve each and every month. If you do miss a goal I want you to catch back that goal the following month so you 100% end up achieving or overachieving your total annual goal.

Below is an example of what you should be tracking.

	Personal Sales Goal	Personal Sales Actual	Difference	Recruits Goal	Recruits Actual	Difference	Team Sales Goal	Team Sales Actual	Difference
January	£	£	Add this number to your next month goal			Add this number to your next month goal	£	£	Add this number to your next month goal
February	£	£	£				£	£	£
March	£	£	£				£	£	£
Quarter Total	£	£	£				£	£	£

	Personal Sales Goal	Personal Sales Actual	Difference	Recruits Goal	Recruits Actual	Difference	Team Sales Goal	Team Sales Actual	Difference
April	£	£	£				£	£	£
May	£	£	£				£	£	£
June	£	£	£				£	£	£
Quarter Total	£	£	£				£	£	£

	Personal Sales Goal	Personal Sales Actual	Difference	Recruits Goal	Recruits Actual	Difference	Team Sales Goal	Team Sales Actual	Difference
July	£	£	£				£	£	£
August	£	£	£				£	£	£
September	£	£	£				£	£	£
Quarter Total	£	£	£				£	£	£

	Personal Sales Goal	Personal Sales Actual	Difference	Recruits Goal	Recruits Actual	Difference	Team Sales Goal	Team Sales Actual	Difference
October	£	£	£				£	£	£
November	£	£	£				£	£	£
December	£	£	£				£	£	£
Annual Total	£	£	£				£	£	£

Be a Product of your Product

Truth Bomb Four

HOW TO BUILD YOUR PERSONAL SALES

Now you've established which company you should be with and got your mindset in order you need to start building those sales.

You will maybe have people say your personal sales are not important – I don't agree. You have to be a product of the product.

If you can't get your own product sales – you don't believe in your product enough. How do you expect to teach your team to drive sales if you can't?

So how do you go about finding lovely, repeat ordering clients?

If I hear "I'm not a salesperson and that's why I can't make my business work" one more time, I think I will scream. You're all able to sell and you are all sold to on a daily basis by people no different to you.

What does it mean to be a great salesperson?

Well, I'll tell you now there is no magic trick the only thing that all great salespeople have in common is the ability to gain trust and build relationships quickly. It doesn't matter what you are buying you have to like and trust the person you are buying from. And what's more if you like them enough you'll keep coming back.

How do you do that I hear you ask. Just be you. You have friends, right? You have a family that loves you? So, you must be a pretty lovely person? Always strive to be 100% you, connect with people however you would in your normal life. Don't try to be someone else or follow someone's script, as that won't work. People will try and tell you that their way works. Don't follow scripts or word choices that are given to you, be YOU. Their script might work for them, but it doesn't mean it will for you. Approach people in a friendly, smiley manner and offer something great and who would say no to that?

Now you may have to do some stuff that pushes you outside of your normal comfort zone so maybe talking to more strangers, posting videos, doing FB lives etc. but remember these people don't know it's outside of your comfort zone and will probably look at you and go 'Wow, she's confident'.

Just be YOU, not an imitation or fake version of what you think you should be in this industry. Don't follow what someone else says you should be doing, be your fabulous self and stay true to your own values. Who wants to be a clone anyway?

Never stop personally selling successfully. You need to be a role model to your team and you also need to find new creative ways that you can feed to them to find customers. You will only find these methods if you are walking the walk.

Stay humble and never be too big for your boots to sell.

So how do you go about finding your lovely customers to build your personal sales?

Now this is where it gets interesting – there isn't one way that works better than any others, so you need to find what works for you.

The reality is your customers are literally everywhere. Be loud and be proud about what you do and what you solve. Talk to as many people as you can. The one thing guaranteed in this industry is that no-one will ever come and knock on your front door and ask to either buy your product or to join your team – your business cannot be a secret.

When you first start out practice your product knowledge on your family and closest friends and ask them to be amongst your first product testers. You want this honest feedback to boost your start and to build your confidence. However, this is not about hassling the life out of your nearest and dearest to get your business started.

Now start gradually networking within your own network, so do your friends work somewhere you could drop some info or samples in. Do your friends have family and friends that may be interested.

Having a launch party to showcase your products when you first start can really kick start your business.

Attend local events and become known in your area as the go to person for your brand.

Use your social media effectively without being too salesy or spammy. We will come onto this in more detail later on. Your business must be visible but visible in a good way. Too many people fall into the trap of annoying the hell out of people on their social. It's always about relationships.

Relationships in the real world and online. Connecting with people is the most important factor in your biz.

Make sure you are completely honest with yourself about what actions you are taking. Keep a daily list of what you have done that is moving you closer to your goals. Action is what is going to make this happen and that is a fact.

You need to focus on your IPA (Income Producing Activities) and finding customers is one of those really important activities.

Keep going – **DO NOT TAKE YOUR FOOT OFF THE GAS**

Your success relies on you continually generating a supply of customer leads.

This Networking list should become a part of your business consistently and should keep growing – if you stop looking for new customers and start just revisiting the same ones over and over people will soon get fed up with you and you will never reach a new audience. Your business will stagnate and eventually stop growing.

Another really important thing to think about is when you build a team your teamies will duplicate what you do, so if you are shockingly bad at your personal sales how can you ever expect them to be great at it? Be the best version of yourself so others aspire to be you.

Use the list on the next page to explore everyone you know. However, do not pre-judge where they may fit into your business. You need to start every conversation with an open mind and no pre-judgment. Don't think how they fit into your business just that you want to talk to them about it.

List your Friends, Family Work Colleagues, Partners network, Kids network (school, clubs etc.), Neighbours, Clubs/Gym, Social Media

This doesn't mean you will suddenly bombard everyone with your products and opportunity but simply gives you a starting point to guide your conversations and make sure you don't miss anyone out!

1	21
2	22
3	23
4	24
5	25
6	26
7	27
8	28
9	29
10	30
11	31
12	32
13	33
14	34
15	35
16	36
17	37
18	38
19	39
20	40

A brand is no longer
what we tell our
customers it is
It's what customers tell
each other it is

Identifying your target audience

You have to know who your audience is so that your branding calls out to the people that you are trying to influence.

This is where it all begins. Don't fall into the trap of trying to appeal to everyone and therefore appealing to no-one. Get really clear about who you are trying to reach out to. Trust me, saying I want everyone to love my products won't cut the mustard.

Take some time to really consider what your perfect customer looks like and then you can tailor your branding, communication and social media to call out to them specifically.

Be as specific as possible and really drill down into who your ideal client is.

You may find this exercise challenging but this will make all the difference to your content when we come to that point. We can be tempted to think we need to call out to everyone, but the reality is when we try and do this, we actually call out to no one – you have to make sure your business calls out to your tribe.

Make some notes below of who your target audience is below.

Gender	
Age Bracket	
Possible Occupations	
Earning Bracket	
Family Life	
Interests	

Getting your branding right

People buy from people not from companies. I have never bought a product because I love the company. It's always been about how it looks, how it makes me feel, whether I liked and trusted the person who is selling it to me.

How you make people feel counts.

Really think about what you want your business to be known for right at the very start?

What are you passionate about?
What are your values?
What do you really enjoy doing?
What makes you unique?

Take some real time over thinking about this. Get your nearest family and friends involved what do they think makes you YOU.

I know exactly what I am about, and I am always true to this and market myself this way.

I'm honest, direct talking, approachable and 100% passionate about Network Marketing and enabling people to change their lives through it using social media and digital marketing responsibly. I always stay true to this and will quickly change my situation if anything conflicts with it

Get Creative. Think about your branding from the point of view of how you want your branding to look and feel to the outside world

Will you have signature colours you use?
A logo?
A Name? (I always advise still using your name too, people need to connect with you and be able to find you easily)
Which platforms will you focus on using most – we'll come back to this one further on in the book

Customer Service is ALWAYS King

Once you have your first customers under your belt you need to look after them properly.

As consumers we have so many opportunities to make purchasing decisions every day so you must stay in the minds of your customers. Whichever brand you join they will have competitors competing for their custom. No one remembers average customer service, but we always remember good or bad! Go the extra mile and be remembered for the right reasons.

After your customer has received their first order take a moment to call or text them to check it has arrived and find out how they are getting on. Give any care tips that are relevant to their product purchase. Diarise when your customer would need to reorder if it is a consumable product. Add ALL customers to a VIP Facebook group so your new customer stays connected with you and can see any special offers that you have running.

Make your customers feel valued; we always remember how people make us feel. In a world of products reviews the last thing you want is any bad press.

I always tell the story of my favourite mascara I buy. I buy it every time through the same business but unfortunately never through the same Consultant in that biz. Every time I purchase it, I patiently wait for further contact from the person I purchased from and EVERY time I am hear nothing so try the next one!

Please don't let me forget you!

Stay in touch, look after me and you will have a customer for life.

Consistent action
=
Consistent results

Truth Bomb Five

GETTING YOUR LIFE BALANCE RIGHT

This business can feel all-consuming and that is not always healthy. You also might be running this business as a side hustle at the start so also working full time and doing this in your spare time.

How do you get the balance you need and how do you run your business well but without peeing off everyone around you.

I'll be honest this is still a work in progress for me. I'm obsessed! I'm not going to lie!

Obsession isn't always a bad word but can be if it is driving the people round you mad. I'll be honest I don't know when to switch off and when I try to, I'm rubbish at it, if that's a thing?

When you are a high performing individual you often struggle to switch off as your brain is always on the run.

I'm sure you get it - everything I have told you so far is about working hard, probably harder than you have ever worked before to reach your goals. I really do believe hard work beats talent every time. If you are the person that just doesn't know when to stop you will always outperform the person with stacks of talent but no drive.

But let's not get this twisted here – burn out gets you NOWHERE.

You have to learn that self-care is also an important part of your journey.

When your phone runs out of battery you re-charge it otherwise it doesn't work anymore. You are just the same.

Now I've been there several times over my own career where I have reached total and utter debilitatating burn out and I'm pretty sure I'll end up there again as it sort of comes with the territory but try and recognise when you need to stop.

Take a breath and re-charge.

If you find yourself up early, late to bed and generally on your biz 24/7 it may be time to take a break as otherwise I guarantee you will hit a wall with it. It will stop being fun, you will struggle to get where you want to be and you will start to feel tired and this will mean you won't be playing at your top level game. This is the time you need to step back, sharpen your axe and re-group.

This self-care recovery leads to creative thoughts which allows you to re-focus, be more present in your business and start to enjoy the process again.

How do you take this time out?

Do something for the whole day absolutely not related to your business, totally switch off, go technology cold turkey for a day and come back refreshed and ready to take on the world.

The reality is hard work AND recovery beats talent not just constant hard work.

The road will have some bumps and there is no fast track option

I told you at the start this was the warts and all version, sorry not sorry.

Your business will not always go the way you want it to but learn to love failure, it teaches us the lessons we need to grow. I really do 100% believe everyone comes into your business for a reason, leaves for a reason and it all happens for a reason. It just doesn't always feel like that at the time. Learn to re-frame your failures as lessons.

And if you are not in it for the long haul and willing to take the rough with the smooth you shouldn't be in it at all. So, pop this book down and go on your laptop and find a job instead.

Success takes time

Growth takes time

You can have everything you want from this industry if you are willing to step up on to the rollercoaster and stay the distance.

Take the rough with the smooth, learn from the bumps, adapt, tweak and move on quickly when someone or something disrupts your journey.

Be patient and stay strong, this thing is going to take some time!

You've got this!

Simple systems create clarity

Managing your Time

TIME IS 100% OUR MOST VALUABLE COMMODITY

Most of us think carefully about how we spend our money, but how many of us put as much thought into how we invest our time?

You can always earn more money, but when the time is gone, it's gone and you can't get it back – ever!

Below are my top tips to manage your time effectively:

1: Grade your Tasks for the day by Importance

You need to learn to analyse every task quickly and effectively to decide whether it is Super Important, fairly important, normal priority or a nice to do.

2: Set a Time Limit for Tasks

Set a time limit to tasks and block out the time required in your diary. Set an alarm on your phone for certain tasks so you don't waste time. You need to get productive with your time particularly if you are fitting this venture round working full time or other commitments that take up a lot of your time. It's particularly important to set an alarm for tasks that can run away with you so as an example Social Media – I am sure we have all lost time scrolling when we didn't need to!

3: Write a clear 'To do list' each morning

All goals and projects are made up of smaller parts that need to be accomplished in order to achieve your goals. Create your 'To do list' round the measurable steps that need to be completed. Life will throw up interruptions during your day that might stop you from completing your list. Be strict with yourself, grade the task that has distracted you and get back on track if you can.

4: It's ok to be imperfect

When you're a perfectionist, nothing will ever be good enough. That means you'll keep going back to same task over and over again. How productive do you think your day will be as a result?

So, stop being perfect. It doesn't exist. Do the best you can and move on.

5: Learn to say no

Set your boundaries and set your shop front out so people know what to expect from you. It is not a bad thing to say no, it is not selfish, it's ok to say no when you need to. You don't have to always be a people pleaser. Trust me I should know I am a recovering one! You are allowing the other person to be responsible for their own life. Honour your truth when you feel like you shouldn't do something, just don't do it, it really is that simple. Practice saying no when you really mean it and it's ok to say 'I'm really time pressed at the moment as I am building my side hustle so my priority at the moment is to dedicate my free time to this'. People will understand if you are honest with them about your priorities and have more respect for you being honest.

6: Complete your most challenging tasks in the morning

Most of us find our first hour of the work day the most productive – make sure to use your first hour wisely! First thing is also most likely the point that you have yet to be distracted by other tasks during the day so it's a great point to get the 'Important Stuff' done with a clear head.

7: Turn off social media app alerts.

The constant ping of social media app alerts are not going to help you be productive with your time. Turn them off. You don't need alerts going through every moment of your day. This will slow you down and hinder your concentration.

8: Use a good Network Marketing Planner

There are some great Network Marketing planners available. Invest in one to help you goal set, manage your prospects and stay on top of your priorities.

9: Make your day longer!

All of us get 24 hours in a day. It's not possible to change the number of hours in a day but you can definitely try waking up a little earlier and make your day longer than it was before. Ideally, your body requires 6–8 hours of sleep to be at your optimum energy levels. The more you adopt a getting up early routine the more you will get used to it. Even if it just setting your alarm 15 minutes earlier, that is 15 minutes you didn't have the day before. Gradually you can increase the number of hours you have in the day to increase your productivity. You might want to use this time for tasks that set you up to have your best day for example meditating first thing or for me it is about being out in nature with my dogs. Whilst we are on gaining more hours – watch how many hours you watch TV. Can you cut this down? This truly is un-productive time. We all need to relax and this is important too but watch that TV isn't taking up time that could be spent on something that moves your business forwards instead.

10: No multitasking

Produce quality work over quantity. I know lots of people who are martyrs to their business. They literally pride themselves on being busy and constantly juggle several tasks at once. Do you recognise yourself here? If so, I have news for you. The latest research suggests that only 2% of people can multi-task effectively. For the remaining 98% of people, multitasking is actually wasting their time and lessening their overall productivity. Instead of dividing your attention between lots of different things, it's better to focus entirely on one thing and do it really well.

Social Media is ALWAYS about relationships

Truth Bomb Six

HOW TO SLAY YOUR SOCIAL MEDIA STRATEGY

I get it, you feel comfortable on Facebook. You know your way around; you feel pretty proficient in using it? If I asked you on a scale of 1-10 how you would rate yourself on FB - you'd maybe put yourself as a 7-8 or even higher?

But my question is do you get the business result you would like from it? Do you get consistent online orders through it?

Maybe, you create in your opinion a great post about your business and then get that icky feeling in the pit of your stomach as you know that once you hit post you will probably get the same result as the other posts about your business - nothing! No reactions, no comments, no share, no online orders.

You then panic that you are annoying your friends and family by posting about your business so before you know it you are a secret agent in your own business i.e. no one evens knows if it still exists and you definitely don't feel equipped to build and engage an audience for it?

Now it's like a Mexican standoff - you want online orders but you don't want to pee your audience off by posting about it.

You can only know what you know, it is that simple. If there is an area of your business that you need to improve on, you absolutely owe it to your business to upskill yourself in that area?

Building an Omni-Channel business is vital to your success in the age we live in now. You only have to look at our changing high streets to know that the businesses that survive are the ones taking an online/offline synergy approach.

What does that even mean I ask you say.

You may have heard of Omni-Channel and maybe also Multi-Channel now they are slightly different.

When a business is Multi-Channel it has several different channels where consumers can purchase products from but it tends to keep the consumer in whichever channel they have chosen whereas Omni-Channel means that all the channels are open to your customers and they can switch and move between channels depending on what suits them and how they want to shop and interact.

It is always about how your customers want to shop not how you want to sell to them.

Adopt an Omni-Channel business where your customers can move between dealing with you in both online and offline, they can shop easily both online and offline but ultimately develop a relationship with you where you are always present so they stick with you creating customer and brand loyalty to you.

Having a strong social media strategy in the direct sales industry is crucial to your success.

The reality is we don't ever visit social media with buyer intent but we are influenced into making purchasing decisions on a daily basis. Social media is the biggest network you will ever tap in to but it needs to be done in the right way to be successful and to deliver consistent results.

I've been using Social Media for my direct sales businesses for well over 10 years, did I do it well in the early days? Probably not! I expect I was a spammy arsehole. You sort of could get away with it back in the day as no-one was using it that much. It was a bit like the Wild West.

However, with the dawn of direct sales businesses that are predominantly targeting Consultants to just use their Social Media you can't get away with being a knob on your Social Media anymore.

You can't really choose whether you use it for Network Marketing now in my opinion only how well you do it! Make sure you get it right from day one and avoid the pitfalls and mistakes I made – back in the day.

So, my two top tips for your social media are:

Tip 1: *Think of your Social Media like the real world*

Use this to police what you do. If you put your activities into a real-life scenario would you still do it?

Let's explore this a little more.

When I say think of your Social Media like the real world. If you wouldn't do something in the real world – do not do it online. Would you knock on a complete stranger's door and say 'buy my stuff or join my team?'

If you were brave enough to do this what do you think the response would be?

Not all that positive I suspect? Do not become a Social Media cold caller.

Take some time to build relationships.

Now think of the same scenario but this time I have taken the time to get to know you. I have reacted to your posts, I've got involved and made a connection.

Now I am no longer a cold caller, I am more like a friendly neighbour? Now when I have a conversation about my business you are far more likely to have a positive response as I have taken the time to form a meaningful connection.

Or

Think of it this way:

Constantly bombarding people with your posts or pushing your products is the equivalent of the pushy salesperson in a shop. You know the one? You walk in and they are instantly on you. What do we do in this situation? We either go to a part of the shop where we can avoid them or leave as quickly as possible as it just feels pushy and uncomfortable. If you make people feel like this in your Social Media trust me people will move away from you at a hundred miles an away.

Tip 2: *Solve me something don't sell me something*

What do I mean by this? You have to make people care about what you do and you have to add value. What does your product or opportunity solve for people? Tap into people's pain points and emotion and they will be far more likely to respond. We love to shop but we hate feeling sold to? Solve something for me and you are no longer selling to me – you are helping me.

Cold caller vs Warm market. No-one wants to be the cold caller and it rarely works anyway so put your Social Media into the real world and use it as your guideline as to whether you should or shouldn't do something.

We are going to explore a method I train people in called Grow, Engage, Convert.

GROW your Audience

ENGAGE with your audience

CONVERT your audience to customers/team members

Let's start at the beginning. The first question I am often asked is which platform should I be on?

The real answer to this one is on which ever one you feel most comfortable on. Try and become s**t hot on at least one rather than not being a master of any of them. I'm predominantly Facebook with a bit of Instagram thrown in.

The first thing I want you to do is to give your Social Media a health check. Try and look at your Social Media with outside eyes.

If I didn't know you what would I think of you?

Would I like and trust you?

Can I even see you and what you are about?

Does your profile create curiosity?

Or do you just look like a carbon copy of the other people from your company?

Your branding should be about you not the company you sell for.

It's all about attracting people that are like you, so therefore I have to be able to see YOU. I spend lots of time with people on courses where I cannot unpick who they are or what they are into from looking at their Social Media. All I see is a series of posts sharing other people's content and nothing about them.

Unless you work for the secret service I want you and what you are about to be highly visible in your Social Media. I can't learn to like and trust you and therefore start a business relationship with you unless I know who you are.

Be present, be likeable and appeal to your target audience.

Use the form below to give your Social Media a bit of a Health Check

Can I see instantly what you do?	Yes No
Does your bio contain relevant links Page/Group/website etc	Yes No
Is your profile picture of you?	Yes No
How often do you post?	Every Day Once a week Once a fortnight. Less
How many Facebook Friends do you have?	
How many likes on your business page?	
How many group members?	
How many Instagram followers?	

Your attitude to your Social Media makes a BIG difference.

I come across people who are not open to changing what they do on Social Media at all. Their Social Media practices are so ingrained in their everyday life that they cannot move away from doing it how they have always done it – even though it is not driving a result for them doing it that way.

Again, if this is you step away from my book.

However, if you would like to learn the insider tips on how to be successful in digital marketing read on. You may need to do some 'Stuff' that moves you out of your comfort zone but that is what is going to grow your business. I'm not here to tell you how to run your business but my methods work so if you are willing to think about your Social Media slightly differently you will move forwards with it and begin to monetise your activity on there.

The most common objections I get from my training sessions are:

I don't want to connect with strangers on my Social Media

That's cool don't grow your audience then, stay just where you are. It really is that simple. If your connections/friends are not growing neither is your network so you are effectively just talking to the same people again and again, over and over. Your Social Media Network will eventually stagnate and you will never be able to move forwards with it.

I don't want people to see my private life

Again, cool but if I'm going to shop or join you, I need to like and trust you. I can't do that if I can't see who you are? You are always in charge of what I do or don't see. It's your profile, you create the life you allow me to see. This is not about creating a 'Disney' life. It needs to be your real, authentic life but you don't need to show me everything for me to feel a connection to you but I have to be able to form an opinion on whether you are my cup of tea or not.

I don't get any interaction when I post about my business

Errrrm your content is the issue not the Social Media platform! Stop talking about your product and start talking about what it solves. Solve me something don't sell me something. Re-read the info earlier. If there is tumble weed every time you post about your business something is not working right in your Social Media strategy.

I don't want to advertise on Social Media

Fab but back in the day you would have been advertising your business in the yellow pages, local newspapers, flyer dropping etc. Social Media advertising is just another tool to reach a new audience. Don't be too quick to write it off, if it's done right it works. We'll come on to this in more detail in a bit.

If you are now thinking yes, I think like that to any of the above statements read on and let's see if we can get you to think about Social Media for your business a little bit differently.

Social Media success takes Commitment, Consistency, a clear strategy and an open mind.

Let's start at the beginning ....

Where to play on Facebook

On Facebook people ask all the time where should I play? Do I need a business page and groups? Should I post on my profile about my business?

Now let's be clear the 3 three things do 3 different things and on the most part most people are using them wrongly.

Your Profile: Your profile is about connecting with new people and building friendships. When someone meets you in the real world they may well go and look you up so first impressions count. Hence the profile health check. I should never feel sold to from viewing your profile, but I should feel curious to find out more. You are not allowed to sell from your profile. You do however need to be growing your Social Media friends or followers for your business to grow. Otherwise you are just stagnating and talking to the same people over and over. Make sure you are growing your connections.

Your Business Page: You invite people across to this page from your profile and it should be value giving for anyone liking/following it. Most people use their business page wrongly and instantly start selling to the people following it.

If I've been friends with you in your profile, learnt to like and trust you and then the second I like your business page you instantly go BAM 'Buy my s**t', not a nice transition?

Think of your business page like a magazine it should be value giving, entertaining and useful to be a part of. You should include interesting articles, free hint and tips, info outside of what the page is about, and I should definitely still feel like it fits your personal branding.

Your groups: I always urge everyone to create a VIP customer group. This is the point where you can actively sell to your audience. I am expecting to be sold to when I join this group so your communication to me can change. Can you see how someone has come through a process before I hit them with my product or opportunity? They now like and trust me; I've given them value for free and then finally said 'hey come and see what I do'. Your group should still over value and should absolutely be about creating a community linked to you. It is a great way for you to offer awesome customer service, so I never miss a deal or special offer as a preferential customer.

GROW – ENGAGE - CONVERT

How to GROW your Social Media audience

To grow your business page and group you first need to grow your audience. Widen the amount of people you are reaching, communicate with more people and create meaningful connections.

Make a commitment to grow your audience on Social Media every day.

How many new connections will you make?

Notice I said connections there.

This is about **'Connecting'** with people not **'Collecting'** people.

Let's start with Facebook first and then we'll come to Instagram as a separate topic.

Use Facebook friend suggestions, they are usually pretty accurate that you would be similar to these people. Connect with them and then send a little message to say 'Hi' along with mentioning any friends you have in common.

Do not just add people for the sake of adding them, that is just a pointless exercise. Make sure the people you are connecting with are like minded and maybe someone you would be friends with in the real world. And please for the love of god do not jump straight into the pitching your business the second they accept your friend request, or you will have them running for the hills.

Join groups that interest you – join and then join in. Give value from getting involved in posts and then begin to connect with the people in the group. Finding the key influencers and connecting with them can really help. Add value in these groups and never spam the members.

Connect with all who connect with you. If someone likes/comments/shares your content send them a little thanks as a private message.

Engage with other people's posts so they start to do the same with yours.

Start to show up in people's notifications so they start to get interested in who you are

Connect with anyone who you are meeting in the real world and bring them into your online world.

There is absolutely nothing wrong when you meet someone saying 'Hey, did you want to connect on Facebook?'. This gives you an opportunity to grow the relationship and stay in touch really easily. If you have your profile working the right way it also gives you a great opportunity to build a bit of intrigue and get them thinking 'Hmmmm I want to play in this person's world, they really have their s**t together'

Your business should always have an online/offline synergy thing going on.

The people you meet in the real world come into your online world and vice versa.

How to ENGAGE with your target audience by creating killer content

Top tips for your content:

Don't make it too generic – it should absolutely call out to your audience you identified a couple of exercises ago. Be hyper relevant to your audience

Get obsessed with serving people – what value are you giving

Solve me something – don't sell me something

We make buying decisions based on emotion – how you make people feel counts

Put yourself in the shoes of your customers

Top 10 Post Types guaranteed to drive engagement

1: Lifestyle (family, pets etc.)

2: Run polls

3: Go Live

4: Text only – under 85 words

5: Milestones reached

6: Before and after

7: Video (time lapse, product how to etc.)

8: Interviews (use Live to interview a friend or colleague)

9: Contests

10. Free content giveaway (cheat sheet, how to etc.)

How often should you post? At least once a day and commit to going live once a week. Live is vital but we'll come back to that in a bit.

Develop a Social Media strategy so you are not getting up every day wondering what on earth to post about. Sit and think about how you can be strategic in your Social Media. Mix the content of your posts up and always analyse what is getting a good result.

Video content is really important to your Social Media. Video is proven to get lots of extra organic reach and live gets even more. Facebook's own studies have found that users stay on a video post for 5 times longer than a static image and 96% of people find video useful in making a purchasing decision. It's all about jolting someone's scrolling and a moving image is a great way to do this.

You can test this theory by beginning to track what reach you get from different posts types in the insights in your business page.

Video gets the most reach, then image and then finally a shared link gets the least. This makes perfect sense as whichever platform you are in does not want you taking their user out of their platform with a link to elsewhere.

Facebook live is really key to your social media strategy. If you feel like you are not brave enough to go live to your audience, get over it! You need to brave and bold in your Social Media and hiding in the shadows will not grow a business. Be imperfectly perfect. Imperfect action always trumps no action at all.

My top tips for a great Facebook Live:

1: Choose your background. It should be attractive and maybe have some product placement without feeling salesy. Test different lighting options to get it just right. Make sure your background screams success and looks professional. Nothing worse than mess in the background of a live

2: How do you come across? Get yourself ready. If I am potentially going to join your team I want to see someone that looks like they have their s**t together not someone who likes like they are losing the plot

3: Have some bullet points near you so you stay on track. Nothing worse than someone rambling in their lives. I instantly stop watching if someone is waffling and you probably do too

4: Practice by making 'Only You' the audience so that you can see how you come across

5: Give people the heads up you will be going live at a certain time

6. Don't spend 10 minutes saying "I'm just going to wait and see who is going to jump on". Just get straight into your content. You will lose anyone who is watching if you spend the first bit waiting for people to come on

7: Don't panic if you can't go live at the same time as answering any questions or comments that come up. Say you will be jumping back on after to reply. You may find you get used to this as time goes by. There is a bit of a knack to it.

8: Thank people for watching and ask if they enjoyed the content to give you a 'Like' or a 'share'

9: Go back in and reply to ALL comments during your live

10: Consider using ones that get a good reaction as advertising to amplify it's reach

Stories

Stories work really well when used properly. I always describe these in my training as a behind the scenes of my live. They don't have to be perfect or polished, it just a little sneaky peek of the workings of your life. It's always really interesting to me that completely different people to react to my stories than to my normal newsfeed so I am reaching a different audience when using my story feature.

Communicating on Social Media

Messenger is a great way to communicate with your potential client base, however, please don't become the person who spams the life out of the people you are connecting with.

YOU HAVE TO BUILD THE RELATIONSHIP FIRST!

I have lost count of the number of times someone friends me and then instantly sends me a message saying

'Hi, thanks for connecting I wonder if you would be interested in XYZ' – Nope not now you have taken that approach or worse still the ones who 'pretend' they are starting a connection with you 'Hi, how's your day going?' Errrrm do I look stupid to you? I instantly think cut to the chase 'what are you going to try and sell me'.

So how do you tackle this in a more meaningful way?

Firstly, build a relationship. Connect with people and then get to know them through their profile. Become their friend, react and comment on their content. Begin to build up a picture of who they are and what makes them tick.

If you meet someone in the real world re-connecting with a little voice message can be really powerful. Far more so than just typing a message. It is great for them to hear your voice again to create that emotional connection with you.

Once you have done the groundwork to build a relationship then and only then would then and only then I would suggest opening a dialogue about your business.

When do you know it's ok to open a dialogue?

When you have had some interactions and a start of a relationship has been formed, you'll know it has happened as the person will be interacting with your posts as well as you interacting with theirs. It's early days but this is a great sign that you are now safe to open a dialogue.

Start your conversation with something you know you have in common.

'Hey XXXXX, I notice you are interested in XXXX. Me too, so great that we have connected on here. How's your day today?'

Try and open a bit of a dialogue.

Next offer to give more info on your business product or opportunity.

Open this with 'Just curious but have you heard of/Used XXXX'

If they are not interested move on but thank them for a lovely chat and stay in touch as sometimes people have to hear or see things several times to peek their interest.

If they show some interest ask 'Can I send you some more info for you to review and let me know what you think?'

Yes, arrange when you will send the info and when you will arrange to get their feedback. So, an example. 'Cool, I'll send you some info across at 8pm. It will take you about 10 mins to watch so shall we say I will contact you at 8.30pm to answer any questions you may have and to see what you think. Does that sound ok?'

If they say no, you've guessed it move on.

If they say yes get back in touch when you said you would and answer any questions they may have. If you don't feel confident in doing this right now jump on a 3-way call with your leader too. This can actually add a bit of gravitas to your meeting.

End the conversation with 'Is there anything else you need to know from me before you would feel ready to get started?'

If they say they are not interested.

'No worries at all XXXX, there was never any pressure from my side I just thought it might have been a good fit for you but maybe not right now? If it's ok with you though can I keep posted on my progress in case you change your mind at some point?'

Never come across as desperate when using messenger and most definitely NEVER be rude to anyone on there. True story I once had a lady send me a barrage of horrible messages because she could see I had read her spammy message but not responded. She told me I would never go anywhere in business if I didn't reply to a message and that I was rude for ignoring her. No love but what was rude was you messaging a complete stranger without ever taking anytime to build a relationship with me and then sending me a sales message when I had clearly made no noises that I was even open to this.

There was also a spate a few years ago of a well know slimming brand randomly messaging people on Facebook that they perceived to be overweight to offer them help. What on earth! As you can already work out this really didn't work, the company in question was outed in the National press for its bad practice amongst its team and if I'm honest is probably still recovering from this many years later.

I am not telling you this story to scare you but to encourage you to use messaging carefully and mindfully. It is great when used the right way but can do a lot of damage when used badly. Build relationships, offer value and listen to what people are telling you.

How to monetise your activity – Convert to customers

Once you have grown your audience and started consistently producing engaging content you can then begin to monetise your activity. Social Media is never a quick win. You have to go through the consistency piece to improve your engagement before you will start to see sales come back from it. In the early days you will maybe feel like what you are doing is invisible but you just have to keep going.

So how do you now turn this activity into sales?

- Make sure your content is engaging and has a call to action

- Make sure I know how to shop in the easiest way possible. If you post about a product ensure you include the specific product URL not just a link to your site

- Private message any fab offers. 88% of people open a messenger message vs. 20% email open rate

- Give awesome customer service so I can't forget you and keep coming back

Does Facebook Advertising work?

I'm asked a lot whether people should advertise on Social Media. In my opinion it is worth the investment. Facebook advertising works in two ways. You can either Boost a post you have already put out there or you can pay to put an Advert together. Either way Facebook has incredible targeting tools to reach the audience that is relevant to you. Think back to the exercise at the start of this book where we identified your target audience persona. Back in the day in our industry you would have been flyer dropping, knocking on doors, advertising in the local paper or yellow pages. Facebook advertising is just the modern-day version of this.

Believe in your #Selfie

Instagram Basics

Firstly, you need to work out if your target audience are camped out on Instagram? Earlier in the book you worked out who your target audience was. Instagram's demographic of user is every different to Facebook's bear this is mind.

71% of users are under 35 and the split in gender is virtually even. An Instagram user tends to be much more likely to both discover and shop for new products on this platform. I guess you could say the Instagram user is much more impulsive.

First up you need to get your account looking right for your target audience.

Why would they follow you?
What vale do they get from you?
Why would they want to play in your world?

This all starts with how your bio and grid appear to them – it's a bit like your virtual business card.

Instagram is a very visual platform, so make it work to your advantage. Using the same signature filter and maintaining the same style of photography will give your posts a consistent style, which helps to make them instantly recognisable as they come through your followers feed.

You identified who your target audience is but now I want you to dig a little bit deeper, so What other products or brands would they be into? Who would your audience look up to in terms of celebrities? This is going to help you find your exact target in Instagram. It's no use you just having a load of randoms or worse still just a load of people in the same business as you following you, trust me they are not going to either purchase your products or join your team. You have to do the leg work to find the people that will be interested. With over 1 billion monthly active users on the platform your audience is in there you just have to find them.

Once you have built up this picture of what they would be into search for what other products would they be into. Next click on the followers in this brand, follow the ones that seem like they would be your target audience and bingo hopefully you will start making connections with people that will have an interest in what you do.

Interact with their content and follow them. This will mean they should go and check you out and give you a little follow back and before you know it your followers and made up of purely people that want to know more about what you do.

Make sure your bio calls out to your target audience. Sell your Instagram profile not your product, we all love to shop but we hate feeling sold to. What would make your audience follow you? What interests them? Engage with your audience's pain points. And it really is ok if it repels some people, I will always encourage you to be a bit Marmite. You can't be everyone's cup of tea and that's ok.

Stories are a really important part of building your brand on Instagram. They are like a behind the scenes of your life. They are less formal and help to build trust with your audience. They don't have to be perfect as they are only there for 24 hours.

How do you create engaging content for your Instagram grid? My advice is be human – not just a business. Your grid should be about you in business not just selling product. Show your product in use, hints and tips, quotes, behind the scenes, personal, journey sharing
Have a theme to your posts including a colour palette and common theming. Whatever them you decide on be consistent with it. Your feed is effectively your business card so how it looks and feels is really important.

Using the right hashtags is really important. Think of hashtags as searchable buckets or categories. As well as using Hashtags that already exist you can also create your own at any time that become uniquely you. Instagram posts allow you to share up to 30 and you should be using as many as possible but definitely over 10. Don't use #s that are too popular so I would recommend under 1 million. Research relevant #s that call out to your target audience. Check out which #s your competitors are using so your content appears in the same place. Save your hashtags in the notes section of your phone so that you can adapt and use when needed.

Instagram Live should be a part of your IG strategy. It helps to drive engagement and makes you stand out from other brands. People need to see YOU to learn to like and trust you. Your followers get a push notification to say you are live so they can jump on and watch.

You need to track whether you are growing your Social Media in the right direction – see the example tracker on the next page. I would advise that you both plan your content in advance and ensure it is growing.

Visit www.jachodges.online to purchase a simple tracker to use.

MONDAY	TUESDAY	WEDNESDAY
MONDAY MOTIVATION	FACEBOOK LIVE	LIFESTYLE POST

THURSDAY	FRIDAY	SATURDAY
POLL OR THIS/THAT POST	VIDEO CONTENT	WEEKEND POST

FACEBOOK FRIENDS	LIKES ON BIZ PAGE	GROUP MEMBERS
MONDAY	MONDAY	MONDAY
FRIDAY	FRIDAY	FRIDAY
INCREASE DECREASE	INCREASE DECREASE	INCREASE DECREASE

FACEBOOK LIVE	INSTAGRAM FOLLOWERS	INSTAGRAM FOLLOWING
VIEWS	MONDAY	MONDAY
REACTIONS	FRIDAY	FRIDAY
SHARES	INCREASE DECREASE	INCREASE DECREASE

What gets measured gets done!

Truth Bomb Seven

BECOME A LEADER YOU WOULD FOLLOW

Once you've got some lovely, loyal customers: how do you now go about finding awesome teamies

I am going to drop this truth bomb straight away!

Most people you will bring into your business will disappoint you, sorry but not sorry. You will thank me for this piece of information further down the line!.

People don't always join you to actually build a business – FACT

They often have no intention of doing the work required – FACT

They will say they will do things that they then won't – FACT

So why do they join?

- They may have joined because they admire or like you

- They want to feel part of a community

- They do want to build a business but remember maybe not the same business as you

How should you build? Wide or deep?

Wide, so direct to you or deep, so coming off the people you have bought in?

You have to build wide first to then build in depth. The depth is what will create the long-term income.

The reality is you won't be able to work with everyone so you should work with the willing. Identify the people who have the potential and have proved they take action.

Let me tell you I am 100% allergic to bulls**t and so are lots of other people

In my opinion to become a leader people will follow, firstly you need to be honest about your own journey

I hate the old adage 'Fake it till you make it'.

Don't be an MLMer who runs around telling everyone you are earning a fortune, working literally a couple of hours a week when you're not. Those around you will pretty quickly work out whether this is true or not and lose all faith in what you are promoting to them if this is not true.

Be honest and authentic with people.

If you are at the very start of your journey, tell people. I

f you are part way through your journey to achieving your goals and have hit a brick wall at times, tell people.

If you have achieved the dream life, tell people (but only if it's true).

People have far more respect for you for being honest than if you blag it.

Whose team would you rather join the one full of bulls**t or the one being honest about where they are and where they are trying to get to. I know which Leader I'd rather follow.

You should be upfront right at the start about asking if they are coachable and willing to partner with you to get their business up and running. If they are not coachable, you will be buying yourself a stack of trouble in the future.

Make it clear to them that they absolutely must be able to chat to people and build relationships whether that is online or offline, if they don't want to do this this is not the industry for them. It is a relationship building business, no-one is going to come to them so work out whether they are up for doing this. You can teach them the skills, but they need to be willing to do the leg work at the start.

You need to share your honest journey with people and reach out to like-minded people to join you

Fall in love with the word 'NO' and learn that often a no is a not now rather than a definite no. Trust me when I say lots of people have said no to me that have then come back to me ages later having watched my journey from the side-lines.

Work out:

Why is your team a great team to join?

What will your teamies get from you?

How can you help and support them?

What skills will you teach them?

How will you attract them?

What value will you give them?

The best way to build your team is to use attraction marketing techniques to get people coming to you. If you have to convince someone to join you, they shouldn't be joining you. Watch out for this! Never convince anyone.

Attraction Marketing – heard of it?

Attraction Marketing is about making yourself the go to person in your industry so that people come and find you not the other way around.

So how do you do this I hear you ask?

Get s**t hot at what you do! Become an authority in your area of expertise. Become someone people want to connect with and make them want to play in your world.

You will never achieve this by being pushy, spamming people or generally hounding the people in your network.

This thing will take some time, but it is worth it in the long run.

Use Facebook lives to give free advice and info

Write a blog and give free help and templates to solve an issue

Share your personal life – why would I aspire to be like you? Share your 'real' life not a Disney version of your life.

Be realistic that not everyone is the same as you.

It's a people business but people will shock the hell out of you. I'll tell you now people aren't always nice, and you will learn quickly the pain of moving on from people who have let you down when you were least expecting it.

People often work to their own agenda even if it means messing with yours.

I'm giving you the heads up that this will happen to you. You will have people promise to order product, to join your team, to help at an event, to attend a meeting that will all promise the world and deliver nothing. You will have people that you thought you had formed a bond with blatantly ignore your calls and messages.

What can you do about it?

Nothing, you can't control another's actions, you may feel wronged and let down but that person in that moment on the other side thinks they are doing the right thing. Learn to let go of what these people do and remember 'Success is your best revenge' wish them well, learn from the experience and move on. Your energy is far better spent on continuing to build your business than wasted it on being angry or worried why the person let you down.

Don't over analyse it, just dust yourself off and carry on.

Communication Skills

Consistent communication with your team is vital. People need to feel supported and like they are a part of something bigger. How you communicate with each part of your business should be segmented and different dependent on which group they are. For example, how you talk to your customers should be different to how you communicate with your leaders.

People also respond to and like to be communicated to in different ways. Have this conversation, particularly with your team. How would THEY like to be communicated with.

Face to Face will always give you the best results. Think about how you can communicate with your team on regular basis in the real world. Maybe a monthly or quarterly meeting could work?

A weekly phone call can make all the difference.

Messenger is a great way to communicate. 88% of people open a messenger message vs 23% email open rate on average. Leaving a messenger voice message is really powerful.

Video calls are the next best thing to face to face meetings. There are lots of free platforms you can use nowadays.

A well-placed text message can really hit the spot so a little text to say well done can mean the world.

Email is probably my least favourite communication method but can be useful if you need to get information across that you need to get your team to read. Maybe follow it up with a little text to say 'There is an important email winging it's way to you'.

Handwritten notes are the bee's knees in terms of making someone feel really appreciated. It's the little things and all that. The art of sending a handwritten, heartfelt Thank You or Well Done can be your superpower. When used at the right time and with the right people.

Set Your Team Standards

Set your team's code of ethics right at the start so there can't be any misunderstandings about your expectations.

That way the ground rules are set at the start reducing the chance of any conflicts in the future about your team's behaviour. So, some things to think about setting out at the start.

If you call and they aren't available. How long is acceptable before a call back, 24 hours? You should not have to chase anyone in your team. Ever.

Team meetings. Expectation to attend whenever possible.

Are they coachable? You will be working in partnership, so they need to be willing to accept your coaching

If they agree to a goal they must be accountable for delivering it. And accountable for explaining why they haven't if they don't.

Honesty. You will be honest with them and they need to be honest back. There is nothing worse than a team member who says what you want to hear and then delivers nothing. Or promises things that they have literally no intention of doing.

Becoming a coach

What does it mean to become a 'Coach'?

I really liked this definition of it "To give (someone) professional advice on how to attain their goals"

This is effectively what you need to do for your team. It is not about you telling them how to do something but rather you are helping them come to their own conclusions making them far more likely to actually take action.

I have worked with some fantastic coaches over my career and the very best ones are the ones where you are given such value from an interaction that you don't even register that you have just been coached – pure genius.

Never ask people to do things you are not willing to do yourself.

As a coach you should strive to be exemplary in everything you do. If you are absolutely dedicated to doing a great job, delivering a result and adding value your team will follow your lead.

The only way you get respect from people is to earn it. Not by talking but by doing. Your team need to know that you are motivated by their success not your own.

It is about listening more than it is talking, try and really actively listen to work out what support your team member needs to reach their full potential. Listen without any sort of judgment on where they currently are.

Their reality is just that, theirs!

Coaching is very different from instructing, training or supporting someone to do something. It is a whole different skillset to become a coach.

If you instruct: You would say "you will do XYZ"

If you train: You would say "this is how you do XYZ"

If you support: You would ask "can I help you with XYZ"

Coaching begins with finding out where they are now, where they would like to get to and identifies the challenges and any obstacles or self-limiting beliefs they may have so you can build a plan that will achieve the right results so more of a

Where are you now?

Where do you want to be? How will that feel?

What might the obstacles be along the way? How will you get there?

How do you start to coach I hear you ask?

Step One: Set the scene for the coaching conversation

"As a member of my team my job is to help you fulfil your full potential in your business. Is it ok if I ask you some meaningful questions about your business to see how I can help you move forwards"

Step Two: Find out their reality right now

"Tell me how this month has gone for you" Or 'Tell me about your _____ right now"

Step Three: Identify what their goal is for the next month

"If you could have the perfect month next month, what does that look like for you? What would you achieve?"

Step Four: Help them Emotionally attach to their goal

"What would _____ (achieving this specific dream/goal) do for you?" "And what else?" "And what else?" "How important would you say this is to you on a scale of 1 – 10?"

Step Five: Help them brainstorm what they will need to do to achieve their goal and what obstacles they may come across

"What is your action plan with steps that will achieve your goal. What challenges might you come across?"

Step Six: Put a time scale on when they will take agreed action and create a sense of urgency

"Are you excited? So, the agreed plan is you are going to do XYZ by XYZ."

Step Seven: Arrange a follow up call when the tasks should be completed to progress the coaching

Your style as a Leader is key

To lead and influence a team you need to understand your own style as a Leader and adapt it accordingly to the needs of your individual team members.

You have to build your credibility as a leader.

Credibility is critical for influencing the behaviour of others. Credibility means being believable, trustworthy and a role model and most importantly keeping to any promises you make to your team.

There are said to be 4 power sources you hold as a great leader:

Position Power – your position with a group. As the upline of your team you will be at the top of the pack. This may also mean you are privy to information the rest of the team doesn't have access to

Knowledge Power – this comes from people's perception they have of your knowledge or expertise on a subject. People are considered to have high levels of expertise if they have a history of prior success in an area

Personality Power – how you conduct yourself around other people. It can be a combination of behavioural and physical traits

Network Power – refers to the number of key people you have access to that you can then introduce your team to or they perceive you can

Your team environment and who to spend time with

It is always about developing a supportive environment for your team where everyone feels as though they are a part of the team. It is also vital that you work with the right people. Don't fall into the trap of spending all your time with your problem children, trust me you will have some.

Develop a strategy using your coaching that puts a value on your time. Set clear goals so that your team members get more of your support and time when they are consistently moving forwards with their business.

Your team members will over time potentially fall into the following categories.

Identifying which category they belong in helps you to decipher where best to spend your time. The reality is sometimes the ones that cause you the most problem or shout the loudest get your attention. Watch out for this!

Bonus Boosters – High performing but very resistant to change. They are good at what they do but don't want to change how they do it. Not always a team player. They already know what they are doing and are extremely hard to coach or change so need little of your time.

Rising Stars – Medium to high performers that are receptive to coaching. They are willing to develop their business but need to learn the skills to improve. Worth investing your time into.

Problem Children – Medium to low performance but not necessarily through their own fault. Needs extra support to upskill in various areas. Invest time but always with a clear outcome attached – do what is required they receive more support.

Lost causes – Low to poor performance. Negative attitude in the team. Highly resistant to change and may not have the ability to grow their business further. Virtually impossible to coach as they see a problem with every opportunity. Does not achieve outcomes set for them. This group can be really unhealthy for your team so be aware of the negative impact they may have. Do not waste time on this group unless they prove they can make positive change

A person who feels appreciated will ALWAYS do more than is expected

Recognition

Recognition is an important part of your business and team morale. People like to feel appreciated; it really is that simple. We all like to know when we have done a good job. It is also important for people to know what they are doing well and where they fit within your team. So, they know who they can strive to be like.

What does good look like in your team?

The personal approach for recognition in my opinion really works. A handwritten note for a job well done can be really effective. It doesn't cost much but can mean the world to a team member.

Have a private group where you can share results and recognise your team for their success. Host a monthly recognition call or shoot a video announcing the top achievers in your team.

Make sure recognition is always based on fact and results – not personal feelings. Ensure you recognise a mixture of indicators so that a mixture of achievers is always pulled out each month. If the same old faces are recognised month after month that can actually have the opposite effect and demotivate people if they feel they can never achieve the recognition.

Think about setting treats for your team that will not only build team spirit but also give you the opportunity to further cement your team's overall goals. This could be a day out, an experience, a weekend away or maybe even a holiday as you grow.

Which ever business you are with they will also hopefully recognise you corporately. Set the tone for your team and ensure you lead from the front and achieve incentives and trips set for you by the company. You should always be the best version of you for your team. You can't expect them to achieve excellence if you don't strive for that yourself.

Flowers grow back
Even after they are
stepped on

Truth Bomb Eight

DEALING WITH UNETHICAL BULLS**T

Ok I am just going to tackle this one head on.

Pretty much every business I have been involved in has exposed me to unethical practices happening in varying degrees.

The worst business being one where the field group were actually opening credit accounts for people without the person knowing and then ordering on those accounts. They people thought they were signing up to a mailing list when in actual fact they were opening a credit account for them. They left people with debt for a credit account they didn't ask to open or even know they had.. Staff were literally bullied into going along with the fraudulent practices by senior managers in the business.

I guess on this subject you have to work out where your moral compass sits.

When I witnessed the scenario above I reported it as that was the right thing to do. Initially I was heralded as a hero for being brave enough to speak out but little did I know that was just lip service and they had no intention of stopping these practices. I was later bullied out of the business and was even told blatantly hat I needed to leave it alone or else. I ended up being diagnosed with stress which was quite a shocker and I have the upmost sympathy for anyone suffering with stress. I used to think this was just an excuse for time off work until I found myself suffering!

During this period, I witnessed the worst of human nature including bullying, lying, cheating and generally harmful, sometimes outright cruel actions.

Ultimately the business involved was not willing to rock the boat enough to cut the cancer out of their practices as it would damage the numbers too much, if they had taken a proper stand that would have meant a lot of their sales managers would have had to have been hauled over the coals and they just weren't willing to take a stand so I ended up being forced out and silenced instead.

Now this is obviously an extreme case of malpractice in this particular business but however small the misdemeanour if it doesn't sit right with you then I still believe you should ALWAYS speak up.

If you are asked to do something that does not feel right, it probably isn't.

Always remember it is your business so no matter what your upline advises YOU to do YOU are always in charge. You have to stay true to your internal guidance system or you will not enjoy your business.

If someone asks you to do something that you are not happy with ask yourself

1) Is it legal?

2) Is it ethical?

3) Does it help me grow my business in an honest way?

4) Is the person asking me to do it because it benefits them?

Avoid the quick fix and look after the people around you in your team. You must protect them from any bad influences and lead from the front with the best practice version of you.

If you get dragged into bad behaviour you can pretty much guarantee your team will go down the same route.

Set your team standards high and always carry yourself in a way that means you can always look yourself in the mirror and be proud of who you are.

You deserve to be aligned with your morals. Don't fall into the trap of being a people pleaser and letting yourself be talked into something that doesn't serve you or your business.

Honour your business with the respect it deserves.

You always choose your morals. If you witness something that is illegal, I would absolutely encourage you to report it to the appropriate authorities.

It has taken me a long time for me to feel at peace with me being labelled a whistle blower. Which by the way should be a positive term but is absolutely not a positive experience in reality.

During my whistle blowing there were people within that business that instantly would have nothing to do with me but there were also a lot who absolutely respected my morals and bravery. These are the people whose opinions matter.

I actually bumped into a top leader from this business recently at an event we had both booked. He came and said to me he was so sorry what happened to me and so were most of the other leaders in the business. He explained that they all knew what was happening and had tried to do their bit to voice their concerns but ultimately it fell on deaf ears. He saluted me for my bravery and wished me all the luck in the world with my own business.

I would 100% rather be known for having really high standards and always doing the right thing than being the person who would do anything and trample over anyone to achieve success. You have to look at yourself in the mirror and know you are a good person – make sure you can.

As your success grows and you become more visible you will also open yourself up to people that are not always very nice and put your business under scrutiny. Whilst most people are absolutely cheerleading you on there are also going to be people on the side lines that are willing you to fail. Particularly females in this business will attack other females normally coming from a place of jealousy. Learn to rise above any unethical behaviour, hold your head high and keep on growing.

Truth Bomb Nine

HOW TO ANALYSE YOUR BUSINESS

This is in my opinion one of the most important chapters in this whole book!

There are some real key areas in your business you need to make sure you are analysing. In Truth Bomb number 3 we talked about goal setting. This should have given you the actuals for the year but there are some other key indicators you need to take care of and ensure they are moving in the right direction.

Track your training

Track your leads

Track your product sales

Track your costs

You need to get serious about looking at the metrics in your business and identify which ones are working.

Do more of the 'Stuff' that works.

Develop systems that other people in your team can duplicate easily. Your business should look simple to attract other people, people need to feel they can do what you do with your support of course.

Firstly, identify what training your team needs and then get good at developing this as time goes on.

When you bring someone into your business what do they need from you? What percentage go on to order.

What percentage are with you in 3 months, 6 months, nine months, a year? If they leave or don't get started - why?

It's your job to find out so you can improve.

Leads are the life blood of your business.

Track your leads effectively. Don't be too quick to give leads to team members. Teach them to fish for their own rather than handing it to them on a plate. You need to breed a team that is empowered and independent from you. Otherwise it will become impossible for you to manage. You will stunt its growth if you do too much for them. They will come to expect it and down tools when they are not provided help constantly. If you do give team members leads ensure it is for a reason or as a reward for action they have taken.

Are your product sales growing?

What is your average customer spend?

The great thing with these indicators is you can influence their outcome using training and marketing. Do you want less people selling at a higher value or more people selling at a lower level? The old quantity over quality question. Really think about this question as it is really important. There are successful businesses built on both strategies. Which one do you want your team to be known for? There is no right answer by the way.

What are you spending on your business? Are you re-investing some of your profit back into it? You should be investing in marketing, advertising, recognition and personal development for both you and your team. Make sure your money is invested in the right places that drive a return.

Learn to duplicate yourself and your business has no limits

Truth Bomb Ten

GO FORTH AND MULTIPLY

An empowered team is ultimately what you are striving for in fact you want people who are better at what you do than You!

You can never tell who the super stars in your business will be.

Develop systems that can be duplicated and multiply yourself again and again.

There is always a ceiling to how much you can do on your own but there isn't when you have people doing the same as you. Surround yourself with motivated, inspired teamies that you can train to build a business designed to tap into what they want from their personal goals.

Go forth and multiply and touch as many people's lives as possible. This industry is incredible and can absolutely be life changing.

I hope this book has maybe inspired you whether you are at the very start of your journey or maybe if you have lost your way.

If you have enjoyed it, recommend it or pass on to someone else and good luck – you are awesome. You have got this!

Connect with me on Facebook:

facebook.com/jachodges.digitalmentor

Visit my Website:

Jachodges.online

Book a course with me here:

jac-hodges-digital-mentor.teachable.com

The best way to predict your future is to create it

Abraham Lincoln

ABOUT THE AUTHOR

Jac Hodges has over15 years' experience in the Network Marketing industry. Having worked her way up in the corporate world she then found her niche mentoring Network Marketers and running Social Media courses across the UK. Jac is hugely passionate about the industry and it's reputation as a mainstream business opportunity and is forever promoting the benefits of being part of the industry.

www.jachodges.online

Printed in Poland
by Amazon Fulfillment
Poland Sp. z o.o., Wrocław

56632942R00059